THE DA VINCI CODE CONTROVERSY

10 FACTS YOU SHOULD KNOW

**By Michael J. Easley and John Ankerberg
with Dillon Burroughs**

Moody Publishers
CHICAGO

TABLE OF CONTENTS

THE FACTS BEHIND THE FICTION

*"What I mean," Teabing countered, "is that **almost everything our fathers taught us about Christ is false.**"* (DVC, 235)

*"The greatest cover-up in human history. **Not only was Jesus Christ married, but He was a father.**"* (DVC, 249)

*"The New Testament is **based on fabrications.**"* (DVC, 341)

*"Jesus' establishment as 'the Son of God' was **officially proposed** and **voted** on by the Council of Nicaea."*

*"Hold on. You're saying **Jesus' divinity was the result of a vote?**"*

*"A relatively close vote at that," Teabing added. . . . "By officially endorsing Jesus as the Son of God, **Constantine turned Jesus into a deity** who existed beyond the scope of the human world, an entity whose power was unchallengeable."* (DVC, 233)

I (John) recently interviewed a pastor who shared the following story regarding a conversation he had with a young woman in a restaurant. When the topic of Christianity came up, she replied, "I can never go to church, having read *The Da Vinci Code*. The church clearly is based on lies."[1]

Upon encountering the controversy of *The Da Vinci Code* book and film, many have asked, "What's the big deal? It's just a novel."

The "big deal" is that Dan Brown's best-selling book and blockbuster film promote a fundamental redefinition of Christianity, the Word of God, and even the Lord Jesus Christ Himself. Already with over forty million copies in print in over forty-five languages, the book's influence has touched nearly every part of the globe. While many would agree that Dan Brown's writing captures the imagination through his page-turning tale, we cannot hide from his inaccurate portrayal of essential Christian beliefs. The "big deal" is that many will read *The Da*

Vinci Code, or see the movie, or simply hear conversations about it and conclude, "It must be true." The "big deal" is that Brown's novel is not merely entertaining—it is a flagrant attack on the core beliefs of biblical Christians.

As Erwin Lutzer accurately commented, "If *The Da Vinci Code* were billed as just a novel, it would be an interesting read for conspiracy buffs who like a fast-paced thriller. What makes the book troublesome is that it purports to be based on facts."[2]

For instance, in the opening page of *The Da Vinci Code,* we are told that though the characters and situations are fictional, the facts included in it are all *true.* Reinforcing this claim during an interview on NBC's *Today Show,* Dan Brown was asked, "How much of this is based on reality in terms of things that actually happened?"

"Absolutely all of it . . . all of the art, architecture, secret rituals, secret societies—all of that is historical fact."[3]

But historical facts are a problem for Brown. One of his main themes is the supposedly secret organization The Priory of Sion. We are told that *"it is one of the oldest surviving secret societies on earth"* (DVC, 113), whose members included Sir Isaac Newton, Botticelli, and Leonardo Da Vinci. But the Priory of Sion was really created in 1956 by a man name Pierre Plantard. In 1993, under oath, he admitted he had made up the whole Priory scheme.

Concerning the religious assertions one *National Review* article addresses the current problem at its heart: "What's at stake in *The Da Vinci Code* is nothing less than traditional Christianity itself. . . . The founder of Christianity had a daughter, Sarah, by Mary Magdalene. If true, this theory would overturn some of the central beliefs of Christians."[4]

Why another book on *The Da Vinci Code?* With many excellent resources on Brown's book, it is an important question to ask. We wanted to bring you a quick, useful tool that can help you discuss the issues in an intelligent, but not overwhelming way. My (Michael's) concern is that many people will read the book or see the movie and wonder, "Is that true?" While this book may help you share what you learn with other friends—we hope it will—we are also concerned that *you* know why you believe what you believe.

When I read the book, I turned often to my computer search engine. As Dan Brown described geographic locations and pieces of art, I used an image search engine to "see" what he was describing. What impressed me was how well he described visual images in writing. The more I read and the more images I searched, the more convinced I became that many well-intentioned people will assume what Brown is writing to be true.

Of course, sensations like *The Da Vinci Code* will come and go. But on a deeper level, how do we—those who believe in, love, and serve Jesus Christ—respond to what often feels like an "attack" on all we hold dear? Our hope is that this book will not only help you to understand Brown's book, but also help you know core truths upon which biblical Christianity is built.

The pages that follow seek to help you better understand the facts behind the fiction. While much has been written on the subject, we believe all Christians must be equipped with these ten facts regarding *The Da Vinci Code* and how to approach it with friends, family members, coworkers, neighbors, and other seekers.

May God richly bless and guide you with *His* truth as you prepare yourself for one of the great spiritual battles of our day.

Michael Easley
John Ankerberg
Dillon Burroughs

FACT #1

The Bible Is Complete and Accurate

"The Bible is a **product of man** . . . not of God." (DVC, 231)

"To rewrite the history books, Constantine knew he would need a bold stroke. From this sprang the most profound moment in Christian history . . . **Constantine commissioned and financed a new Bible**, which **omitted** those **gospels** that spoke of **Christ's human traits** and **embellished** those **gospels** that made **Him godlike**. The earlier gospels were outlawed, gathered up, and burned." (DVC, 345)

"The New Testament is based on **fabrications**." (DVC, 341)

Welcome to the world of *The Da Vinci Code*! Could such statements be based on fact? Unfortunately, many have wholeheartedly bought into *The Da Vinci Code*'s idea that much of the Bible includes later editing that created the text and beliefs we hold today. However, when we cross the line from fiction to facts, we quickly discover that the claims made in Dan Brown's best seller are just that—fiction.

One reason we may feel frustrated about challenges like *The Da Vinci Code* is that we do not know how we received the Bible. How was the Bible created, written, and handed down over the generations? If challenged by a friend or coworker about the Bible's origins, would you have the basic information to explain what you believe?

If you are unsure of how to respond, you're not alone. A recent study revealed that fewer than 24 percent of American

Christians can accurately answer key questions regarding core Christian beliefs.[5] So to help in our understanding of how the Bible originally came about, let's discover what is not true and what is true about the Bible as addressed in *The Da Vinci Code*.

THE FICTION

*"The Bible . . . has evolved through countless translations, additions, and revisions. History has **never had** a **definitive version of the book**."* (DVC, 231)

The Da Vinci Code claims that Emperor Constantine attempted to destroy any gospel records that differed from his choices, but that the Dead Sea Scrolls and Nag Hammadi texts preserve additional information about Christ. Nothing could be further from the truth.

First, many documents called the Dead Sea Scrolls were discovered between 1947 and 1956. These extremely well-preserved documents—many complete sections and literally thousands of fragments—are ancient Hebrew texts written before the life of Christ.[6] (The most remarkable is a complete copy of the book of Isaiah on display in the Israel Museum, Jerusalem.) Considered by scholars a major discovery for Old Testament research, these scrolls include some of the earliest manuscripts of many Old Testament Bible books. Their most significant contribution to historical research has actually been to confirm the accuracy of other Old Testament texts handed down by Jewish rabbis. *The Da Vinci Code's* claim that these scrolls contained extra gospels is impossible, since they were written approximately two hundred years *before* Jesus lived in Israel. *The Da Vinci Code* is either wrong—or lying. Constantine would likely have not even known they existed.

Second, the Nag Hammadi[7] documents were Gnostic[8] texts containing religious writings from over a hundred years after the earthly life of Christ. Most were written by authors other than those claimed by each book. No critical scholars agree that the *Gospel of Thomas*, for instance, was actually written by the apostle Thomas. Between AD 100 and AD 250, several books were written with the name of an apostle attached to them to lend a stamp of authenticity to the writing.

Third, the historical works on the Council of Nicaea never mention arguments over which books to include in the New Testament or disputes regarding other Gnostic books. In fact, only two people of the over three hundred in attendance disagreed on the final decision regarding the Nicene Creed. This could hardly be called a conspiracy!

What *The Da Vinci Code* Says...
And What Really Happened ...

The Da Vinci Code Says . . . "Constantine commissioned and financed a new Bible, which omitted those gospels that spoke of Christ's *human traits* and embellished those gospels that made Him godlike." (DVC, 345)

What Really Happened . . . The four gospels were all written by AD 95. The Gnostic writings emerged from AD 150–225. Constantine commissioned Eusebius to have fifty copies of the New Testament made from writings accepted over two hundred years earlier. There was no vote or discussion on this at Nicaea.

The Da Vinci Code Says . . . "Fortunately for historians . . . some of the gospels that Constantine attempted to eradicate managed to survive. The Dead Sea Scrolls were found **in the 1950s** hidden in a cave near Qumran in the Judean desert." (DVC, 234)

What Really Happened . . . Brown is wrong. The Dead Sea Scrolls were **found in 1947.** They contained Old Testament books and were written as many as two hundred years before Christ's birth. These books could not be gospels, since they existed before Jesus even lived on earth.

The Da Vinci Code Says . . . "These documents [the Gnostic Codices] speak of Christ's ministry in very human terms." (DVC, 234)

What Really Happened . . . The Gnostic stories actually speak of Jesus as one of many divine beings more than the physical Jesus. His human body was seen as evil, something that trapped the divine spark. The divine Jesus needed to escape His material body.

THE FACTS

"All Scripture is God-breathed and is useful for teaching, rebuking, correcting and training in righteousness, so that the man of God may be thoroughly equipped for every good work."* 2 TIMOTHY 3:16–17

"Since I myself have carefully investigated everything from the beginning, it seemed good also to me to write an orderly account for you, most excellent Theophilus, so that you may know the certainty of the things you have been taught."* LUKE 1:3–4

So if the Bible didn't emerge from conspiracy and political motives, how did it come into being? First, we must recognize that the Bible is unique among all the ancient books of the world. The Bible was written by forty authors over a period of 1,500 years. To find the Bible without error and in agreement in its essentials can only be explained through God's supernatural intervention.

How did the twenty-seven New Testament books come down to us and result in the present form? Everything starts with Jesus. Most scholars hold that Jesus' earthly ministry began when He was in His late twenties. He chose twelve apostles to follow Him and learn from Him over a three-year period. The New Testament books are intimately connected to the Twelve: those who walked with Jesus.

WHO WROTE THE NEW TESTAMENT?
The twenty-seven books have nine basic sources.

Two apostles, Matthew and John, wrote gospels. John also wrote three letters and Revelation. Peter authored two letters and was a source for Mark's gospel. Peter also recognized Paul's writings as Scripture (2 PETER 3:16).

Luke based his gospel on the eyewitness testimony of the apostles. He was also a traveling companion of the apostle Paul. Paul later quotes Luke's gospel as Scripture in 1 Timothy 5:18.

James and Jude were human brothers of Jesus. James did not believe Jesus was the Christ until after Jesus rose from the dead and appeared to him personally. James later became bishop of the Jerusalem church and wrote the New Testament book of James. Jude believed after the resurrection as well, writing the book that bears his name.

The author of Hebrews was well-known to the recipients of his teachings, but not to everyone in the early church, which delayed the epistle's immediate acceptance. Many claim the author was Barnabas, a fellow missionary with Paul. Others believe Apollos wrote it during his early year with Paul in Corinth. Whoever wrote the book of Hebrews had direct contact with an apostle.

Nine individuals wrote the twenty-seven books received by the churches as Scripture. All the New Testament books were written approximately AD 50 to 80. Only John's gospel was written in the 90s, but all of these books were received by different church congregations and in circulation before AD 95. Within approximately one generation of the New Testament's completion, every book had been cited by a church father.[9] In AD 367 Athanasius wrote an authoritative list of these twenty-seven books.

World-renowned scholars affirm that the Scriptures were not mishandled or mistranslated as they were copied and handed down. After examining and comparing the New Testament documents with other books of ancient history, Sir Frederick Kenyon, formerly director and principal librarian of the British Museum, stated:

> In no other case is the interval of time between **the composition of the book** and the date of the earliest extant [**the oldest texts that exist today**] manuscripts so short as in that of the New Testament. The interval, then, between the dates of original composition and the earliest extant evidence become so small as to be in fact negligible, and the last foundation for any doubt that the Scriptures have come down to us substantially as they were written, has now been removed. **Both the authenticity** and the **general integrity** of the **books of the New Testament** may be regarded **as finally established.**[10]

When *The Da Vinci Code* suggests the Bible's final content was decided on at Nicaea, it's untrue. All but two of 318 church leaders held to the divinity of Jesus as worded in the Nicene Creed. The real reason these church leaders gathered was to settle a dispute with Arius, a man who argued that Jesus was a created being rather than the Creator of all things. This assertion stood in opposition to the apostles, including John, who wrote, "In the beginning was the Word, and the Word was with God, and the Word was God. He was with God in the beginning. **Through him all things were made; without him nothing was made that has been made**" (JOHN 1:1–3). If He is Creator, then He could not create Himself. In staying true to the apostles' teaching, these bishops affirmed that Jesus was of the *same* nature as God rather than a *similar* nature.

How do we know the books in the Old Testament are from God? Norman Geisler presents the case about the facts of the

Old Testament this way:

> Jesus taught definitely that God was the originator of the Hebrew Old Testament. He taught as authoritative or authentic most of the books of the Hebrew canon ... he asserted that the Old Testament as a whole was unbreakable Scripture (JOHN 10:35); that it would never perish (MATTHEW 5:18); and that it must be fulfilled (LUKE 24:44) ... Jesus not only defined the limits ... but he laid down the principle of canonicity.[11]

In Matthew 5:17–19 Jesus speaks of the inspiration of God's Word in the Old Testament.[12] "Inspiration," notes Charles Ryrie, "is ... God's superintendence of the human authors so that, using their own individual personalities, they composed and recorded without error His revelation to man in the words of the original autographs." Several additional New Testament passages affirm this teaching.[13]

When researching the New Testament, you will find that the number of early texts far exceeds that of any other work in history. The earliest fragments of the gospel of John emerge from within one generation of the apostle John's life (approximately AD 125).

In total, over 5,300 Greek texts (the original New Testament language), 10,000 Latin texts, and 9,300 other versions exist from the early history of the church. In comparison, of sixteen well-known classical Greek authors, the typical number of early copies is *fewer than ten*, with the earliest copies dating from 750 to 1600 years *after* the originals were written.

Outside of the New Testament, several additional early writings connect with the events of historic Christianity. The second generation of Christianity includes eight clear sources supporting its authority.

WHY ARE THE CHURCH FATHERS IMPORTANT?

The church fathers were first-, second-, and third-generation church leaders and followers of the apostles who personally served with Jesus. In addition to spreading the teachings as taught directly from the apostles, they help affirm the acceptance and accuracy of the New Testament text from frequent references in their writings. For instance, Irenaeus (AD 170) quoted twenty-three of the twenty-seven New Testament books less than a hundred years after the writing of the New Testament books, meaning that he had access to this many books together within a generation of the apostles. This would have been a tremendous accomplishment for a culture whose writings could only be spread through handwritten copies! Some of the early leading church fathers (and sources) include . . .

1. CLEMENT. He was a leading elder in the church at Rome. In his epistle to the Corinthians (AD 95), he cites portions of Matthew, Mark, and Luke, and introduces them as the actual words of Jesus.

2. PAPIAS. He was bishop of Hierapolis in Phrygia and author of Exposition of Oracles of the Lord (AD 130), citing the gospels of Matthew, Mark, Luke, and John, presumably as accepted works. He specifically refers to John's gospel as containing the words of Jesus.

3. JUSTIN MARTYR. He was the best-known defender of Christianity in the second century (AD 140) and considered all four gospels to be Scripture.

4. THE DIDACHE. This served as an ancient manual of Christianity that dates between the end of the first century and the beginning of the second century. It cites portions of the first three gospels, referring to them as the words of Jesus, and quotes extensively from the gospel of Matthew.

5. POLYCARP. A student of the apostle John, he quotes portions of Matthew, Mark, and Luke, referring to them as the very words of Jesus (AD 150).

6. IRENAEUS. A student of Polycarp (AD 170), he quotes from twenty-three of the twenty-seven New Testament books, omitting only the shortest New Testament books such as Philemon and 3 John.

7. THE MURATORIAN FRAGMENT. Dating to about AD 175, it includes Matthew, Mark, Luke, and John as the four gospels. In total, this list includes twenty-three of the twenty-seven New Testament books.

8. PAPYRUS 45. This fragment, dated around AD 200, includes all four gospels together. [14]

New Testament Greek scholar Kurt Aland comments that the New Testament "was not imposed from the top, be it by bishops or synods, and then accepted by the communities.... The organized church did not create the canon [New Testament]; it recognized the canon that had been created."[15]

But just how were the New Testament books selected? How can we know that these books are accurate and reliably the Word of God? The basic historical rules that guided recognition of the canon are as follows, listed in question format:[16]

1. **Was the book written or supported by a prophet or apostle of God?** This was the most important factor. The reasoning here is that the Word of God which is inspired by the Spirit of God for the people of God must be communicated through a person of God. Second Peter 1:20–21 assures us that Scripture is only written by God's people. In Galatians the apostle Paul argued support for the book of Galatians by

appealing to the fact that he was an authorized messenger of God, an apostle.

2. **Is the book authoritative?** In other words, can it be said of the book as it was said of Jesus, "The people were amazed at his teaching, because he taught them as one who had authority, not as the teachers of the law" (MARK 1:22). Put another way, does this book ring with the sense of "The Lord says . . ."?

3. **Does the book tell the truth about God consistent with previous revelation?** A group called the Bereans searched the Old Testament Scriptures to determine whether Paul's teaching was true (ACTS 17:11). They knew that if Paul's teaching did not resonate with the Old Testament writings, it could not be of God. Agreement with all earlier revelation was essential (GALATIANS 1:8).

4. **Does the book give evidence of having the power of God?** Any writing that does not exhibit the transforming power of God in the lives of its readers could not have come from God. Scripture says that the Word of God is "living and active" (HEBREWS 4:12). Second Timothy 3:16–17 indicates that God's Word has a transforming effect. If the book in question did not have the power to change a life, then the book could not have come from God.

5. **Was the book accepted by the people of God?** In Old Testament times, Moses' scrolls were immediately placed into the ark of the covenant (DEUTERONOMY 31:24–26), as were Joshua's (JOSHUA 24:26). In the New Testament, Paul thanked the Thessalonians for receiving his message as the Word of God (1 THESSALONIANS 2:13). Paul's letters were also circulated

among the churches (COLOSSIANS 4:16; 1 THESSALONIANS 5:27). It was common that the majority of God's people would initially accept God's Word.

But what exactly is canonicity? Geisler writes, "Canonicity refers to the normative or authoritative books inspired by God for inclusion in Holy Scripture. Canonicity is determined by God. It is not the antiquity, authenticity, or religious community that makes a book canonical or authoritative. A book is valuable because it is canonical, and not canonical because it is or was considered valuable. Its authority is established by God and merely discovered by God's people."[17] Or, to put it another way, "God determined the Canon and man discovered it."[18]

Far beyond Dan Brown's deceptive allegations against the Bible, it is an amazingly consistent book. Multiple authorship, hundreds of years of compilation, thousands of additional documents stretched across time and geographic places, again and again prove the Bible's reliability and consistency.

In speaking with others about Scripture in relation to *The Da Vinci Code*, try the following:

✓ ASK LEADING QUESTIONS:
"How much of *The Da Vinci Code* do you feel is accurate? Why?"

✓ REFER TO SCRIPTURE:
"How much of the Bible have you read yourself?"
"What do you think about it? Are there parts you don't understand?"

✓ KEEP COMMUNICATION OPEN:
"The next time I see you, let's talk about how some of the people and events in the Bible fit together."

FACT #2

Jesus Never Married

"The marriage of Jesus and Mary Magdalene is
part of the historical record." (DVC, 245)

•

"The Last Supper *practically shouts at the viewer that*
Jesus and Magdalene were a pair." (DVC, 244)

•

*"The early Church needed to convince the world that the mortal
prophet Jesus was a divine being. Therefore, any gospels that
described earthly aspects of Jesus' life had to be omitted from the
Bible . . . . One particularly troubling earthly theme kept recurring
in the gospels. Mary Magdalene . . . more specifically,
her marriage to Jesus Christ."* (DVC, 244)

During a recent interview on the controversy surrounding *The Da Vinci Code*, I (John) was shocked to hear Erwin Lutzer share the following personal story from his congregation: "A friend of mine works at a financial institution. She called up and she said, 'Mr. Lutzer, you have to understand something. People are reading *The Da Vinci Code* in my office. And some of them are Christians, and they're coming away asking whether or not at least a part of it is true. Could Jesus really have been married to Mary Magdalene?"[19] The short answer is this. If you read all three hundred volumes of the Christian church fathers, each volume consisting of hundreds of pages each, and read all of the writings contained in the Gnostic library, you will find absolutely no evidence that says Jesus was married to anyone.

But in *The Da Vinci Code*, Dan Brown's character, Teabing, claims that Jewish custom expected that every man marry, including Jesus. Celibacy was condemned. He cites the *Gospel of Philip* as his proof for Christ's marriage relationship, quoting:

> "*The companion of the Saviour is Mary Magdalene. Christ loved her more than all the disciples and used to kiss her often on her mouth. The rest of the disciples were offended by it and expressed disapproval. They said to him, 'Why do you love her more than all of us?'* " (DVC, 246)

The Da Vinci Code suggests this passage proves that Mary Magdalene was the companion of Jesus. It also claims that in Aramaic, "companion" means "spouse." This is not true. As Paul Maier points out:

> Crucial segments of the passage Brown will cite are missing in the manuscript, since the first line actually reads: "And the companion of . . . Mary Magdalene . . . her more than the disciples . . . kiss her . . . " Yet Brown bravely translates the subject as Jesus (who, by the way, may have kissed only her hand). And "companion," Brown renders as "spouse or wife in Aramaic."[20]

The problem with Brown's assertion in *The Da Vinci Code* is that the *Gospel of Philip* wasn't written in Aramaic; it was written in Coptic.[21] The word "companion" is borrowed from Greek. New Testament scholar Ben Witherington says it most likely means "sister."[22] Within this context, it likely suggests a spiritual relationship.[23] According to Darrell Bock, research professor of the New Testament at Dallas Theological Seminary, the term for "companion" is not even the typical term used for wife.[24]

Can you begin to see the problems associated with such sources? The *Gospel of Philip* never actually says Jesus was married. Worse, this source dates to about AD 275, two hundred years after the writing of the traditional gospels. Could a book written so far removed from the event suddenly announce such a profound secret not mentioned in earlier gospels? When looking at the details, the novel doesn't even include the correct original language.

THE FICTION

> *"The marriage of Jesus* and Mary Magdalene is
> part of the historical record." (DVC, 245)

Where does Dan Brown obtain his proof for a married Jesus? Some try to argue that since it was expected of every Jewish man to marry, then surely Jesus must have married at some point. However, this argument has the following weaknesses:

1. Several highly esteemed Jewish and Christian spiritual leaders remained single—including the prophet Jeremiah, the apostle Paul, and John the Baptist. Entire religious communities of the time included unmarried men, among them the Essene community in Qumran.
2. Jewish leaders often granted exceptions to the general rule of marriage. It was certainly not an unchangeable requirement.

The only other historical reference made regarding this issue by Brown's character Teabing is from the *Gospel of Mary Magdalene*. However, this document is also of late origin. The historical Mary Magdalene did not author its contents. In contrast to Teabing's statement, "I shan't bore you with the countless references to Jesus and Magdalene's union" (DVC, 247), the *Gospel of Mary Magdalene* itself does not even claim a marriage between Jesus and Mary!

One final claim *The Da Vinci Code* makes suggests that the figure to the right of Jesus in the famous painting *The Last Supper* is actually Mary Magdalene rather than the apostle John. Lutzer writes, "The notion that Mary Magdalene rather than the apostle John is seated to the right of Jesus is rejected by most art historians. . . . When you look at the picture, you might agree that John, sitting to the right of Jesus, looks effeminate, but such a depiction was consistent with other portraits of him in Florence."[25]

THE FACTS

Let us rejoice and be glad and give him glory! For the wedding of the Lamb has come, and his bride has made herself ready. . . . Then the angel said to me, "Write: 'Blessed are those who are invited to the wedding supper of the Lamb.' . . . These are the true words of God." REVELATION 19:7–9

The only marriage linked to Jesus in the New Testament declares a future marriage of Christ (the Lamb of God) and the church in Revelation 19.

In contrast, the deafening silence in the twenty-seven books of the New Testament and the vast majority of early Christian writings refute the erroneous claim that Jesus was married:

- The Bible never mentions Jesus being married prior to the beginning of His three-year ministry.
- It never mentions Jesus being married during His three-year ministry.
- It never mentions Jesus being married at the crucifixion.
- It never mentions Jesus being married at His burial.
- It never mentions Jesus being married at His resurrection.

Consider, too, Paul's writings about marriage. It's noteworthy that he mentions a wife for Peter and the other apostles—and not for Jesus. In 1 Corinthians 9:5 Paul defends his right to get married if he chose to do so: "Don't we have the right to take a believing wife along with us, as do the other apostles and the Lord's brothers and Cephas?" If Jesus had been married, this would be a logical place for Paul to cite Jesus' marriage as the number-one precedent.

The temptation accounts, where Jesus is in the wilderness for forty days and forty nights, also offer a clue.[26] In those vulnerable and weak days, Satan tempts Him in key areas that would dismantle His work as Messiah. The gospels record Christ's perfect resistance to temptations, even when hungry, weak, and tired. This strongly suggests that as He always does what pleases His Father, only does what His Father tells Him, and was perfectly obedient in every way (JOHN 8:29), it is simply an invention to suggest He covertly married.

Last, would it make "biblical sense" to have the sinless, perfect Son of God, sent to redeem sinful mankind, marry a sinful woman? What redemptive, theological purpose would this accomplish? If it were part of God's plan that His Son be married while on this earth, it would have been clearly revealed in Scripture. Every aspect of Jesus' life is deliberate and in perfect obedience to the Father. In the future, Jesus Christ will marry His bride, the church. While scholars debate the figurative or literal nature of this wedding, it seems convincing that even if it were a figurative image, Christ would have to be the perfect, sinless, and single man to be married to the church He redeemed with His blood (REVELATION 19:7–9).

Clearly, the evidence is against Jesus being married when He lived on earth. When dialoguing with others on the issue of whether Jesus was married, ask:

✓ How likely do you think it is that Jesus married someone when He lived on earth?

✓ If Jesus did marry, why do you think no one would mention it in the gospels or other early Christian writings?

✓ Does it make a difference in your view of Jesus whether He was married or not?

FACT #3

Christianity Did Not Emerge from Mystery Religions

"Nothing in Christianity is original." (DVC, 232)

·

*"The vestiges of pagan religion in Christian symbology are undeniable. Egyptian sun disks became the halos of Catholic saints. Pictograms of Isis nursing her miraculously conceived son Horus became the blueprint for our modern images of the Virgin Mary nursing Baby Jesus. And virtually all the elements . . . **were taken directly from earlier pagan mystery religions.**"* (DVC, 232)

The Da Vinci Code claims that Christianity is an unoriginal invention, heavily borrowing from pagan "mystery" religions. For example, some argue the virgin birth of Jesus is nothing more than a retelling of Greek mythology. Yet such assertions blur the distinctions between the two stories. In Greek mythology, male gods would come down and have sex with human women to give birth to hybrid beings. This is not what happened with Jesus. Jesus was born as the Son of God in earthly form, a God-man rather than a hybrid. In contrast with Greek mythology, the birth of Jesus was also predicted nearly seven hundred years before its occurrence (ISAIAH 7:14), long before these Greek mythologies were developed.

But could Christianity, in some small way, really be borrowing from other religions, rather than revealing the plan of the one true God? Again, in researching *The Da Vinci Code*, several distinctions between fiction and fact emerge to reveal the truth of the matter.

THE FICTION

> "**Nothing in Christianity is original.** *The pre-Christian God Mithras*—called the Son of God and the Light of the World—*was born on December 25, died, was buried in a rock tomb, and then resurrected in three days.*" (DVC, 232)

Is Christianity really unoriginal as this quote suggests? What about this Mithras? Who was he? Did his story really parallel the story of Jesus?

Mithras was an ancient Persian god who was worshiped by Indian Aryans and Zoroastrians, as well as by various followers in Rome. To further confuse the history of this god, the religion's followers did not keep written documents, instead passing on their traditions through secret practices and rituals. In fact, manuscripts of the mystery religions claiming a dying and rising God are dated from the second century after Christ. Erwin Lutzer writes:

> The Christian faith is deeply rooted in historical fact rather than mythology. The cult of Mithras was continually evolving and historically hard to pin down; its legends varied from one era to another and from one locale to another. What seems most probable is that the specific myths about Mithras's miraculous birth and becoming a "savior god" were modeled after the stories of Jesus.[27]

But have other religions claimed a resurrection story similar to the story of Jesus? The historical evidence points to these stories as nothing more than urban legends. One authority asks, "Which mystery gods actually experienced a resurrection from the dead? . . . One can speak of a 'resurrection' in the stories . . . only in the most extended of senses. For example, after Isis gathered together the pieces of Osiris's dismembered body, Osiris became 'Lord of the Underworld.' This is a poor substitute for a resurrection like that of Jesus Christ. And, no claim can be made that Mithras was a 'dying and rising god.' " [28]

It would appear, then, that the real mythology lies not in the origin of Christianity but in the minds of skeptics who are confusing such beliefs with the historical person and work of Jesus of Nazareth.[29]

THE FACTS

"Almost all of our sources of information about the pagan religions alleged to have influenced early Christianity are dated very late. We frequently find writers quoting from documents written 300 years [later]."[30]

If Christianity, especially the life of Jesus Christ, is not derivative from other beliefs but distinctly different in its claims, in what ways is Christ truly unique? The Bible provides six specific areas:[31]

1. **The Predictions of His Coming:** The fact of fulfilled prophecy is a unique feature of Christianity. No other religious system can claim such accuracy.

What Predictions?
+ The birth of Jesus Christ
+ His family history
+ How He would be born
+ Where He would be raised
+ His work
+ His purpose
+ His death
+ His resurrection

These predictions were all recorded hundreds of years before the earthly birth of Christ. In his book *Science Speaks*, Peter Stoner applies the modern science of probability to eight prophecies concerning Christ. He says, "The chance that any man might have . . . fulfilled all eight prophecies is one in 10 to the 17th. That would be 1 in 100,000,000,000,000,000" (one hundred quadrillion).[32]

2. **The Nature of His Birth:** The birth of Jesus was unique in all human history. No other religious story comes close to the narrative of the birth of Jesus Christ prior to His time. By the miraculous work of the Holy Spirit, God entered a virgin's womb so that after a natural nine-month pregnancy, she gave birth to a son who was also God's Son. As a result of this unique birth, Christ was born without sin, would die on the cross as the sinless and perfect sacrifice, the Lamb of God, and will reign on the throne of His father David as the Lion of the tribe of Judah (REVELATION 5).

3. **The Uniqueness of His Person:** The Bible claims that Jesus is both God and man. This is found in the unified divine and human natures of Christ—two natures united in one person. As God He created all things (JOHN 1:1). As man He was sinless, entering as the perfect substitute for humanity's sin. Jesus was completely man and completely God in one person.

4. **The Uniqueness of His Life:** His life is unparalleled in character and impact. No one spoke like Jesus Christ, performed the miracles He did, or made the claims He made. In view of Christ's powerful words and works, the claims He made cannot be dismissed.

5. **The Uniqueness of His Death:** His death is also unique, not because He was crucified, but because His specific death was prophesied in Psalm 22 long before death by crucifixion was even known in Israel. His death is also unique because He died as a sinless and perfect man, unlike any person before or since His time. Third, His death is unique because of the miracles surrounding His death—a total eclipse, an earthquake, and the opening of graves. After watching the events of that day, the Roman centurion on the scene believed, "Truly this was the Son of God." (MATTHEW 27:54, NLT).

6. **The Uniqueness of His Resurrection:** Many spiritual leaders have come and gone, but none have come back from the dead to carry on their work like Jesus Christ. The Old Testament predictions, the empty tomb, His post-resurrection appearances, the transformed lives of His disciples, and the perseverance of Christianity through extreme persecution all help confirm the power and uniqueness of His indestructible life. Literally hundreds were eyewitnesses of His resurrection.

The facts of the Christian faith withstand the attacks of those who disagree. When *The Da Vinci Code* claims in its opening page that "*all* descriptions of artwork, architecture, documents, and secret rituals in this novel are accurate," we must note that these words, too, are only fiction.

As C.S. Lewis wrote, "Jahweh [God] is clearly not a Nature-God. He does not die and come to life each year as a true corn-king should. . . . He is not the soul of Nature nor any part of Nature. He inhabits eternity; he dwells in the high and holy place; heaven is his throne."[33]

As you talk with others about the uniqueness of Jesus Christ and the roots of Christianity, ask these questions:

✓ How much do you know about the connections between the Old Testament and the New Testament?

✓ How do you think the world would be different without the existence of Jesus Christ? How would your life be different?

✓ How much have you investigated the life of Jesus?

✓ Would you consider reading through some of the teachings of Jesus in the gospels with me?

FACT #4

The Hidden Gospels Are Not Really Gospels

"Fortunately for historians," Teabing said, *"**some of the gospels that Constantine attempted to eradicate managed to survive.** The Dead Sea Scrolls were found in the 1950s hidden in a cave near Qumran in the Judean desert."* (DVC, 234)

*"The Coptic Scrolls [were found] in 1945 at Nag Hammadi. In addition to telling the true Grail story, these documents speak of Christ's ministry in very human terms. . . . **The scrolls highlight glaring historical discrepancies and fabrications**, clearly confirming that the modern Bible was compiled and edited by men who possessed a political agenda—to promote the divinity of the man Jesus Christ and use His influence to solidify their own power base."* (DVC, 234)

These documents define what mystics believe. Gnostics believed they had access to mysteries or advanced knowledge other Christians did not possess. This gnosis (from the Greek word for "knowledge") centered on completely different teachings about God and creation, the person of Jesus, His work on the cross, salvation, man's problem (not sin, but ignorance), and Christ's role in the world.

Here's where the problem begins. The Dead Sea Scrolls and Nag Hammadi documents have been tremendous sources for Christian research, but are these texts "survivors" of early Scriptures Constantine had attempted to destroy? If not, what are they?

If these discoveries truly do reveal information hidden by the early church, their influence would be quite remarkable. We who follow Christ would crave as much knowledge from them as possible. However, *The Da Vinci Code* greatly exaggerates the truth of these documents, providing another source of fiction for Brown's writing and yet another need for us to examine what is true concerning the history of these ancient texts.

THE FICTION

*"More than **eighty** gospels were considered for the New Testament, and yet only a relative few were chosen for inclusion—Matthew, Mark, Luke, and John."* (DVC, 231)

What About the Dead Sea Scrolls?

Is there any truth to the idea that the Dead Sea Scrolls, Nag Hammadi texts, and over eighty gospels were deceptively excluded from our New Testament?

According to Norman Geisler and hundreds of other credible scholars, the Dead Sea Scrolls confirm the reliability of the Old Testament. The Dead Sea Scrolls were stored in clay jars and hidden in mountain caves in an area called Qumran near the Dead Sea. They include significant portions of key Old Testament books that were copied and studied by a sect known as the Essenes. These manuscripts date from as early as the third century before Christ.

By studying these scrolls, scholars have found that the "scrolls give an overwhelming confirmation of the faithfulness with which the Hebrew text was copied through the centuries."[34] But confirmation of the Old Testament is not the only benefit the Christian church has derived from this amazing cache.

But "the Dead Sea Scrolls in no way provide proof that any secret gospels exist. Instead, they confirm the accuracy of the New Testament books and the historical background of the time reflected in the New Testament books."[35]

What about the Nag Hammadi Documents?

But what about the mysterious Nag Hammadi documents? Upon investigation, we find that most of these texts consist of later works termed Gnostic gospels.

> The Nag Hammadi Texts . . . are named after the place they were found on the west bank of the Nile. A library was found containing forty-five texts written in the Coptic language. These were written from the early second century to the fourth century AD. Examples of texts included the *Gospel of Thomas*, the *Gospel of Philip*, the *Acts of Peter* and others. These texts were Gnostic in character and found in a library of Gnostic works. [36]

Some early Gnostic ideas were labelled false doctrines by the first-century church. The claim that such works are secret gospels shows a lack of legitimate research. The church and others have known of these documents for centuries. Irenaeus (AD 130–200) and Tertullian (AD 160–225) mentioned the texts in their letters along with their rejection of them. None of the Gnostic texts were ever considered part of the inspired writings of the apostles.

What about the Eighty Lost Gospels?

What about the other eighty or more "lost gospels" cited in *The Da Vinci Code?* Is there any evidence that they existed? The answer is clearly no. Craig Blomberg writes:

> Another blatantly fictitious portion of *The Da Vinci Code* is the claim that "more than eighty gospels were considered for the New Testament." Add up everything

that was ever called a gospel in the first half-millennium of Christianity (most of which are small compilations of esoteric sayings ascribed to Jesus and not narratives of any portion of His life) and you come up with about two dozen documents. [37]

So what is the evidence that these hidden gospels provide better historical information about Jesus than that which is in our New Testament? There is none. The facts are that the biblical gospels existed earlier, carry much greater manuscript evidence, and hold the backing of church leaders from even the earliest times.

THE FACTS

For I testify to everyone who hears the words of the prophecy of this book: **If anyone adds to these things, God will add to him the plagues that are written in this book;** *and if anyone takes away from the words of the book of this prophecy, God shall take away his part from the Book of Life, from the holy city, and from the things which are written in this book.* REVELATION 22:18–19 (NKJV)

In contrast to the claims of *The Da Vinci Code*, the apostle John writes in Revelation that those who changed God's Word could expect severe consequences. The earliest Christians believed in God's Word so strongly that they would never have made intentional changes to Scripture.

The Dead Sea Scrolls do comment with great insight into the tremendous efforts given to copying Scripture. These copyists knew they were duplicating God's Word. They went to incredible lengths to ensure that no error crept into their work. The scribes carefully counted every line, word, syllable, and letter to guarantee accuracy.

In addition, in these scrolls discovered at Qumran in 1947, we have Old Testament manuscripts that date to about a thousand years earlier (150 BC) than the other Old Testament manuscripts previously in our possession. When the two sets of manuscripts are compared, they were essentially found the same, with very few differences. The fact that manuscripts separated by a thousand years are essentially consistent indicates the incredible accuracy of the Old Testament's tradition.

The copy of the book of Isaiah discovered at Qumran illustrates this accuracy. Gleason Archer, who personally examined both the AD 980 and BC 150 copies of Isaiah, comments:

> Even though the two copies of Isaiah discovered in Qumran Cave 1 near the Dead Sea in 1947 were a thousand years earlier than the oldest dated manuscript previously known (AD 980), they proved to be word for word identical with our standard Hebrew Bible in more than 95 percent of the text. The 5 percent of variation consisted chiefly of obvious slips of the pen and variations in spelling.[38]

In the end, we see that the so-called extra gospels are fantasy stories and not historical gospels at all. Those books accepted from the earliest times in the church have continued to be accurately handed down for each generation to read, understand, and live out in their day.

In speaking with others about *The Da Vinci Code*'s claims of extra or hidden gospels, ask:

✓ What do you think of *The Da Vinci Code*'s claim that there were several other gospels that the early church intentionally hid?

✓ Which parts of the four gospels have you read for yourself? What did you think of them?

FACT #5

Constantine Didn't Invent the New Testament

"Constantine commissioned and financed a new Bible, which omitted those gospels that spoke of Christ's human traits and embellished those gospels that made Him godlike. The earlier gospels were **outlawed, gathered up, and burned.***" (DVC, 234)*

"The modern Bible was compiled and edited by men who possessed a **political agenda** *... to solidify their own power base [in reference to Constantine]." (DVC, 234)*

After Jesus and the apostles, early Christians began to contend for their faith by writing apologies[39] and other books whose goal was to explain and defend Christian truth. In refuting the false views that surfaced, early Christians were forced to explain their own doctrinal statements in increasingly precise terms. When Arius's heretical (false) teaching began to spread in AD 311, the controversy and need for clarification resulted in the gathering of 318 bishops from across the empire at the Council of Nicaea in AD 325.

What was Constantine's role? According to Teabing in *The Da Vinci Code*, Constantine never actually became a Christian, but remained a pagan his entire life and used Christianity for his own political ends. He supposedly gathered the bishops together at the Council of Nicaea in an attempt to unify Christianity. Further, Constantine supposedly compelled those present at the Council to acknowledge that Jesus was divine rather than a "mere human," forcing the Council to create a new Bible which taught this brand-new concept of Christ's divinity.

Scholars who study the history of Christianity will find Teabing's account of history very bizarre. The majority of historians and critical scholars recognize that Constantine saw himself becoming a Christian at least in some sense in AD 312. It is historically true that he tried to unify his new empire behind Christianity, but not in 325 as Teabing says. This occurred shortly after Constantine's conversion in 312. This can be seen by his Edict of Milan in 313, freeing Christians from official government persecution and providing freedom of religion for all people in the empire.

At the Council of Nicaea the bishops did not gather to vote on the divinity of Jesus as Teabing claims. Just the opposite is the case. Every bishop at the Council of Nicaea and nearly every Christian of the time held that Jesus was the divine Son of God. They did not vote on Christ's divinity. Instead, a creed was written. The debate was not whether Jesus was divine, but how was He divine and human? Further, how could Jesus and God both be God if there is only one God? The answer the bishops gave constitutes the Nicene Creed. At the conclusion of the Council, the bishops had the choice of either signing the creed or not. Over three hundred signed it, two did not, and a few others initially abstained but later signed the creed.

Theologian Harold O.J. Brown writes, "His [Constantine's] power and prestige certainly influenced the rapidity of which the council fathers reached the decision, but the nature of that decision was the result of their own deliberations and political maneuverings."[40]

Steve Brandt further supports this view when he writes: "The account of Eusebius fairly glows in regard to the Emperor, and he is portrayed as a key figure. *It is nowhere suggested, however, that he was permitted to vote with the bishops nor that he used any form of force to obtain an outcome.*"[41]

No one needs to worry about what took place at the Council of Nicaea. When the evidence is evaluated, *The Da Vinci Code*'s accusations in this area are simply historically false.

THE FICTION

"Who chose which gospels to include?" Sophie asked. . . .

"Fortunately for historians," Teabing said, **"some of the gospels that Constantine attempted to eradicate managed to survive.** . . . *The Vatican, in keeping with their tradition of misinformation, tried very hard to suppress the release of these scrolls."* (DVC, 231, 234)

Is it true that Constantine produced the Bible as we know it today? Did he destroy earlier documents that tell only of the human Jesus? Do the Dead Sea Scrolls and scrolls and codices of Nag Hammadi tell the true story of the Holy Grail (that Mary Magdalene was Jesus' wife)?

Bart Ehrman, professor of religious studies at the University of North Carolina and an acknowledged authority on the Gnostic library at Nag Hammadi, answers these questions. While Ehrman no longer embraces traditional Christianity, his comments as a historian at this point are quite insightful:

"Unfortunately, much of what Teabing says is historically inaccurate. 1) As we will later see, Constantine did not attempt to eradicate any of the earlier Gospels. 2) The Dead Sea Scrolls do not contain any Gospels, or in fact any documents that speak of Christ or Christianity at all; they are Jewish. 3) Their (initial) discovery was in 1947, not the 1950s. 4) The Coptic documents at Nag Hammadi were in book form, they were not scrolls (an important distinction for the history of early Christian books). 5) Neither these nor the Dead Sea Scrolls ever speak of the Grail story. 6) Nor do they speak of Jesus' ministry "in very human terms"; if anything, Jesus is portrayed as more divine in the Nag Hammadi sources than he is in the Gospels of the New Testament. 7) The Vatican had nothing to do with covering up either of these discoveries."[42]

F.F. Bruce describes how the canon of Scripture was recognized long before Constantine ever lived:

> The first steps in the formation of a canon of authoritative Christian books . . . appear to have been **taken about the beginning of the second century**, when there is evidence for the circulation of two collections of Christian writings in the Church.
>
> At a very early date it appears that the four Gospels were united in one collection. They must have been brought together very soon after the writing of the Gospel according to John. This fourfold collection was known originally as "The Gospel" in the singular, not "The Gospels" in the plural; there was only one Gospel, narrated in four records, distinguished as "according to Matthew," "according to Mark," and so on. . . .
>
> One thing must be emphatically stated. The New Testament books did not become authoritative for the Church because they were formally included in a canonical list; on the contrary, *the Church included them in her canon because she already regarded them as divinely inspired*, recognizing their innate worth and general apostolic authority, direct or indirect.[43]

THE FACTS

> *But know this first of all, that no prophecy of Scripture is a matter*
> *of one's own interpretation, for no prophecy was ever made by an*
> *act of human will, but men moved by the Holy Spirit*
> *spoke from God.* 2 PETER 1:20–21 (NASB)

Once again, did Constantine create a new Bible? The historical answer is no. What did Constantine ask Eusebius to do? Lutzer summarizes, "What Constantine did . . . was commission the historian Eusebius of Caesarea to make fifty Bibles, to be copied onto good parchment by trained scribes for use in the churches of Constantinople."[44]

Which books did he include? According to F.F. Bruce, "The answer is not seriously in doubt. The copies contained all the books which Eusebius lists as universally acknowledged . . . in short, the same twenty-seven books as appear in our copies of the New Testament today."[45]

In discussing the development of the New Testament with others, try asking the following questions:

✓ How much do you know about the origins of the New Testament?

✓ Do you think it's possible to "prove" that all of the New Testament is accurate?

✓ If the message about Jesus Christ in the gospels is accurate, how should that change the way we live now?

FACT #6

Faith Is Not Built on Fabrication

*"Every faith in the world is based on **fabrication**." (DVC, 341)*

*"That is the definition of faith—acceptance of that which we imagine to be true, that which we **cannot prove**." (DVC, 341)*

What is faith? Are the world's religions all based on fabrication? Is faith merely something we imagine is true, but cannot prove?

How is Christianity different from all the other religions in the world? Contrary to the claims in *The Da Vinci Code*, Christianity is based on a real person who lived in real history—Jesus Christ. Christianity allows every person who is searching for truth to examine the facts and evidence before placing his or her faith in Christ.

Jesus Christ was born and raised in a literal town, taught people that He was God, died a literal death and literally rose from the dead. As Udo Middelmann writes, "Faith is not a substitute for knowledge, but the response to it."[46]

THE FICTION

*"By officially endorsing Jesus as the Son of God, **Constantine turned Jesus into a deity** who existed beyond the scope of the human world." (DVC, 233)*

*"Those who truly understand their faiths understand **the stories**"*

are metaphorical. . . . And living in that reality helps millions of people cope and be better people." (DVC, 342)

Here again, what *The Da Vinci Code* claims is false. As we have seen, the Christ of Christianity is solidly rooted in historical fact.

THE FACTS

But what is true faith? And where does Jesus enter into all of this? Defining "faith" is very important. A helpful way to understand "faith" is to think in simple, practical terms. When I (Michael) say "I believe" in something, what do I mean? If I say I believe Cindy when she says, "I love you," what I mean is that I trust her. It is not a feeling. It is a trust based on her word. I have the benefit of trusting her because of our relationship, our commitment, our experience. When a person trusts Christ, believes in Him, and places faith in Him, he or she is saying, "I believe what Jesus says because of who He is and because He is trustworthy."

It is helpful to keep the ideas of faith, belief, and trust together, because that is the sense the Bible has when it tells us of faith. We are believing in something. We are believing in Jesus Christ.

In John 5:24 we read, "Truly, truly, I say to you, he who hears My word, and believes Him who sent Me, has eternal life, and does not come into judgment, but has passed out of death into life" (NASB). Jesus is saying that when we respond to what we *hear* about Him, when we *believe* Him, we are given eternal life.

This kind of faith, belief, trust is not mere acknowledgment. It's not like saying, "Oh, yeah, I believe you." It is embracing the truth of Christ—that He lived, died on the cross, and rose from the dead. It is trusting Him to do for you what you can never do for yourself.

An old story is told of a tightrope walker performing across Niagara Falls. In front of a crowd, he jumped up on the wire and walked from the Canadian side to the American side and back again. He then put a wheelbarrow on the wire and filled it with two hundred pounds of sandbags. He successfully took that wheelbarrow with the sandbags across the falls and back. He asked the crowd, "How many of you think I could place a person in this wheelbarrow and take him across the falls? Raise your hand." All raised their hands. He then asked, "Who will be the first to get in?" No one would trust him with his life.

Jesus asks us, "Do you believe I am the Son of God who died for your sins, the One who can forgive you and offer you eternal life?"

You say, "Lord, I believe."

Then Jesus says, "Then get into My wheelbarrow." Faith is trusting Christ and Christ alone to do for you what you cannot do for yourself. When you trust in Him, God promises, "And the testimony is this, that God has given us eternal life, and this life is in His Son. He who has the Son has the life; he who does not have the Son of God does not have the life" (1 JOHN 5:11–12, NASB).

In terms of Christ saving us, it is not dependent upon how "much" faith we somehow exercise; it has to do with *whom we have faith in*. When I (Michael) had a job as a mechanic, I often encountered a problem I could not repair. After I exhausted my ability, I would go and ask Rayburn, who was an exceptional mechanic at the shop. Whatever he told me was always correct. He was an expert. I learned early on that I could have faith in Rayburn to know how to fix any mechanical problem. It was not about "how much" faith I had in Rayburn; it was "Rayburn is worth my faith because he knows how to fix anything."

God is not looking for some "quantifiable" amount of faith, and unless you have "enough" faith you cannot have eternal life. Rather, He is asking you to believe in Jesus Christ, to have faith in Him. It is not the amount of faith; it is where you place your faith—in Christ. And right now, maybe you feel led by God to entrust yourself to Jesus. If so, admit to Him that you are a sinner and can't save yourself. But from this moment on you're trusting Christ to be your Savior. If you will pray and entrust yourself to Him, He will save you.

Biblical faith is not irrational, but is built upon what God has revealed to us about His works, His character, and His person, through such means as:

1. **History:** In many ways, God has communicated knowledge of Himself through the years and events of historical experience. The Bible is largely a historical account of God's interactions with real people— Abraham, Isaac, Jacob, Mary, Paul, Peter, and John. The greatest example in Old Testament history was the deliverance of Israel from Egypt. God, through Moses, inflicted ten plagues on the Egyptians that demonstrated His awesome power (EXODUS 7–12). Throughout history, God made sure that when a significant event occurred there was a prophet at hand to record and interpret it—Moses at the exodus, the apostles with Jesus.

2. **The Life of Christ:** For God to fully do and say all that He wanted, it required him to leave His eternal residence and enter the arena of humanity. This He did in the person of Jesus Christ. Jesus was God's ultimate "special" revelation. Jesus—as eternal God—took on human flesh so He could be God's "fullest" revelation to humanity (HEBREWS 1:2–3). Jesus was a revelation of God not just in His person as God but also in His life and teachings. By observing the things Jesus did and the things Jesus said, we learn a great deal about God. For example, God's awesome power was revealed in

Jesus (JOHN 3:2). God's incredible wisdom was shown through Jesus (1 CORINTHIANS 1:24). God's boundless love was demonstrated by Jesus (1 JOHN 3:16). God's incomprehensible grace was shared through Jesus (2 THESSALONIANS 1:12).

These verses serve as the background behind why Jesus told a group of Pharisees, "When a man believes in me, he does not believe in me only, but in the one who sent me" (JOHN 12:44). In another situation, Jesus told Philip that "anyone who has seen me has seen the Father" (JOHN 14:9). Jesus served as the ultimate historical revelation of God.

3. **The Bible:** In this one book, God has provided eternal principles He wants us to know about Him and how we can have a relationship with Him.

God is the One who caused the Bible to be written (2 TIMOTHY 3:16; 2 PETER 1:21). Through it He speaks to us today just as He spoke to people in ancient times when the words were first given. The Bible is to be received as God's words to us and honored accordingly. As we submit to the Bible's authority, we place ourselves under the authority of the living God.

In speaking with others about the reality of faith, ask:

✓ What are some of the ways the Christian faith is built upon historical facts?

✓ Can a person have a "reasonable faith," one based in real-life events?

✓ How much evidence should a person have before believing in something they cannot see?

FACT #7

Christianity Embraces the Rights of Women

*"Powerful men in the early Christian church 'conned' the world
by propagating lies that devalued the female and tipped
the scales in favor of the masculine."* (DVC, 124)

Did the early Christian church really "con" the world through lies into thinking of Christianity as a masculine religion that devalues women?

While some contemporary scholars assert that Jesus and the early church were vastly opposed to women's rights, education, and values, the biblical and historical record reveals quite the opposite. One writer argues:

> Jesus most assuredly was not a feminist in the modern sense of the word. He did, however, reject those cultural norms that put women in a disrespected place as second-class citizens of the Kingdom. He countered the expectation of the rabbis by elevating women to a place of honor and influence.[47]

It must be acknowledged that those who call themselves followers of Christ have not always obeyed the Lord in living out His teachings—and example—in this area. Women have been mistreated on many occasions throughout the history of the church, whether through discrimination, neglect, or severe mistreatment. Yet these abuses do not negate the true message of Christianity, calling for the equal status of women and men in the eyes of God and His creation.

THE FICTION

"Constantine and his male successors successfully converted the world from matriarchal paganism to patriarchal Christianity." (DVC, 124)

The Gnostic Gospels—those *The Da Vinci Code* claim were "secret"—actually portray women negatively. Saying 114 of the *Gospel of Thomas* reads:

> Simon Peter is portrayed as saying to Jesus, "Let Mary leave us, for women are not worthy of life." Jesus responded: "I myself shall lead her in order to make her male, so that she too may become a living spirit resembling you males. **For every woman who will make herself male will enter the Kingdom of Heaven.**"[48]

Among the Gnostics in general, women were viewed as incomplete and inferior beings. Many of the so-called lost gospels were written from this perspective. In fact, women could be enlightened and reach true spirituality only by a return to maleness, according to these beliefs. Researcher Edwin Yamauchi comments that Jesus' response to Peter in this quote from the *Gospel of Thomas* "refers to the ultimate reunification of the sexes, as the Gnostics maintained that the separation of the sexes was responsible for the origin of evil."[49]

The Da Vinci Code has it backwards. The Gnostic texts supposedly banished by the church really taught patriarchal ideas, while Christ and the authors of the New Testament elevated the status of women.

One additional passage from *The Da Vinci Code* that stands out in this area is when Dan Brown writes, "Jesus was the original feminist" (248). While it is true that Jesus held women in high regard, to label Him a feminist by some of today's extreme standards is a distortion. This is especially the case in the context of Brown's book, where he connects the feminism of Jesus with the idea that Mary Magdalene was intended as the head of the early church.

The fiction behind the facts regarding Brown's account of Christianity's treatment of women is truly bizarre. The very sources cited as proof for the church's mistreatment of women are actually the documents that speak most poorly of women's rights.

THE FACTS

There is neither Jew nor Greek, there is neither slave nor free,
there is neither male nor female; for you are all one in Christ Jesus.
(GALATIANS 3:28, NKJV)

So God created man in his own image, in the image of God he
created him; male and female he created them. (GENESIS 1:27)

Paul's words to the Galatians underline the fact that a person's race or nationality, or whether they might be free or a slave, a man or a woman, does not change his or her value before God. All who are in Christ have equal value. In a Jewish culture where women were discouraged from formal education, Jesus addressed women right alongside men as equals (MATTHEW 14:21; 15:38). As He taught, He often used women's activities to illustrate the character of the kingdom of God, such as baking bread (LUKE 13:20–21), grinding corn (LUKE 17:35), and sweeping the house to find a lost coin (LUKE 15:8–10).

Some Jewish rabbis taught that a man should not speak to a woman in a public place, but Jesus not only spoke to a woman (a Samaritan woman at that) but accepted a cup of water from her in a public place (JOHN 4:1–30). After He rose from the dead, the first people Christ appeared to were women, not His male disciples or any other men (MATTHEW 28:8–10). Sisters Mary and

Martha appear frequently in the gospels and were clearly some of Jesus' closest friends.

And in the very beginning of the Bible, in the account of creation, God made both man and woman in His image (GENESIS 1:26). Note, too, that in Scripture God's compassion and affections are occasionally described in feminine terms. For example, Jesus likened God to a loving—and saddened—mother hen crying over the waywardness of her children (MATTHEW 23:37–39). God is also said to have "given birth" to Israel (DEUTERONOMY 32:18). Yet Jesus continually referred to God as His Father.

In discussing these issues, ask:

✓ How do you think Christianity portrays women?

✓ Have you ever read what the Bible says about women from the Bible itself? Would you like to? (If so, use some of the verses above and offer them a copy of this book.)

FACT #8

Sex Was Not a Method to Communicate with God

*The sex act enables one to "achieve gnosis—
knowledge of the divine."* (DVC, 308)

*"Mankind's use of sex to commune directly with God posed a seri-
ous threat to the Catholic power base. It left the Church out of the
loop, undermining their self-proclaimed status as the sole conduit to
God. For obvious reasons, **they worked hard to demonize sex
and recast it as a disgusting and sinful act.**"* (DVC, 309)

D id the early church really work to "demonize sex," making
the sexual act a shameful practice? If so, when did this
occur? What historical sources prove these claims? There are
none.

As *The Da Vinci Code* is fiction, adding an elaborate layer of
sexual intrigue cannot but help the sales and hype the controversy.
After all, "sex sells!"

Sexual content in movies and books can be offensive in and
of itself, but our concerns go beyond that. Brown's assertions
strike at two core Christian affirmations. First, we are told sex
is the "real way" to communicate with God. If so, this stands in
complete contrast with the Bible's teaching that we are to come to
God through Christ's atoning work on the cross. Fundamentally,
the idea of sex as a religious or cultic communication with God
violates all of the Bible's teaching on sexual purity.

Second, *Da Vinci* accuses the early church of labeling all sex as evil. The Bible does not teach that sex is evil. Rather, God created sexual intimacy for man and woman to fully enjoy within the context of marriage.

THE FICTION

"The natural sexual union between man and woman through which each became spiritually whole . . . had been **recast as a shameful act.***"* (DVC, 125)

The male "could achieve a climactic instant when his mind went totally blank and he could see God." (DVC, 309)

Sex is "a mystical, spiritual act . . . [in which one can] find **that spark of divinity that man can only achieve through union with the sacred feminine.***"* (DVC, 310)

"Holy men . . . now feared natural sexual urges as the work of the devil." (DVC, 125)

From the quotes above, it is clear *The Da Vinci Code* presents a blatantly false view of sex, one that caters to the spirit of our age. The source of much of Brown's writing in this area draws from the ancient *hieros gamos*, a pagan practice. The *Britannica Concise Encyclopedia* explains the practice as:

> (Greek: "sacred marriage") Sexual relations of fertility deities enacted in myths and rituals, characteristic of societies based on cereal agriculture . . . At least once a year, people dressed as gods engaged in sexual intercourse to guarantee the fertility of the land. The festival began with a procession to the marriage celebration, which was followed by an exchange of gifts, a purification rite,

the wedding feast, preparation of the wedding chamber, and a secret nocturnal act of intercourse.[50]

In other words, *hieros gamos* was a coupling of a god and a man that often included a symbolic pagan religious meaning. Brown's depiction of early Christianity is fabrication, with no historical basis.

THE FACTS

> *Marriage is to be held in honor among all, and the marriage*
> *bed is to be undefiled; for fornicators and adulterers*
> *God will judge.* (HEBREWS 13:4, NASB)

Christianity (as well as Old Testament Judaism) never taught that sex outside of marriage was an acceptable practice. The facts fall along two lines of basic biblical understanding:

1. **The church has not recast sex as a shameful act.**
   Sexual intimacy itself, within its intended context, is a wonderful blessing God has given. (SEE GENESIS 2:24; MATTHEW 19:5; 1 CORINTHIANS 6:16; EPHESIANS 5:31.)

   In Genesis, sexual intimacy was a part of God's "good" creation. The apostle Paul reaffirmed this understanding that God created sex and that "everything created by God is good" (1 TIMOTHY 4:4)— but within the context of the marriage relationship (1 CORINTHIANS 7:2) that God ordained.

   The Song of Solomon illustrates how much God approves of sexual intimacy between a man and woman within marriage. In this dialogue, the conclusion is that God desires a married man and woman to have truly exciting and fulfilling sex.

Christians are taught to abstain from sex outside of marriage (ACTS 15:20). Paul felt so strongly about this that he warned his readers to "flee" wrongful sexual practices (1 CORINTHIANS 6:13, 18). Certainly the sex ritual described in *The Da Vinci Code* of a couple surrounded by a chanting religious group falls outside the teachings of Judaism and the Christian faith.

People of all ages have ventured into all kinds of sexual immorality. The lie promoted in *The Da Vinci Code* or by guilt-free sexual revolution proponents proves the dead end of such escapades. In fact, if these kinds of sexual experiments and expressions satisfied, men and women would not continue in more and more exploits. From God's perspective, sexual intimacy is a precious, powerful, wonderful expression of communication, enjoyment, and procreation for a husband and wife. It is tragic that—again—Dan Brown desecrates that which God has made holy.

2. **Sex was never intended as a means of spiritual growth.** To suggest sex serves as a means for spiritual maturity or obtaining special revelation and knowledge does not come from God's Word. This is another part of Gnosticism's teaching that sexual acts could help one attain a secret knowledge of God.

These corrupted ideas began to surface even in the late New Testament period. They provoked Jude to write the early church to "contend earnestly for the faith which was once for all delivered down to the saints" (JUDE 3, NASB). This "faith" referred to the teachings handed down by the apostles and early church leaders, derived directly from what Christ proclaimed. Any new practices being promoted for a secret knowledge of God, sexual or otherwise, were quickly condemned by the early church.

In exploring the issue of how sex is portrayed in *The Da Vinci Code*, consider asking:

✔ What do you think the Bible really teaches about sex?

✔ In what ways do you think Christian teachings could help in the way our culture views sexual relationships today?

FACT #9

Mary Magdalene Was Not Intended to Replace Peter

"The rock on which Jesus built His Church—was not Peter—
it was Mary Magdalene." (DVC, 248)

Was Mary Magdalene the original choice of Jesus as leader of the church? If so, what evidence backs this up?

This is just more of *The Da Vinci Code's* make-believe history. The truth is that history reveals nothing to support this assertion. The above quote alludes to Matthew 16:18. In this verse Jesus did not claim that Peter was the rock upon whom the church would be built. Rather, Jesus was saying that He Himself is the rock[51] upon which the church would be built.[52] In other words we might paraphrase it, "You are Peter, a rock, but upon this Rock—Me—I will build My church." Peter refers to Christ as "the cornerstone" of the church and to Christians as "living stones" in the church (1 PETER 2:4–8). There can only be one head of the church, and the head is Jesus Christ. Paul understood that "Christ is the head of the church, his body, of which he is the Savior" (EPHESIANS 5:23).

THE FICTION

"Jesus intended for the future of His Church to be in
the hands of Mary Magdalene." (DVC, 248)

This specific claim in *The Da Vinci Code* misrepresents the information found in two historic texts. The first is a Gnostic text from the *Gospel of Mary*. One writer argues:

> The evidence for this [DVC] claim comes largely from the *Gospel of Mary*, which was written by an unknown author in about the second century. It affirms that Jesus loved Mary more than the other disciples. . . . The historical reliability of this story is questionable, but even if it were true, it says nothing about Jesus' intention to build the church on Mary.[53]

Other language scholars have recognized the same inaccuracies of attributing the *Gospel of Mary* as evidence for Mary's role as the church's first leader. Darrell Bock notes,

> What is important to understand about this reading of the *Gospel of Mary* is that the story is not about Peter and Mary at all or about gender roles. They symbolize the dispute over revelation. . . . It confirms that **the real fight was about who receives revelation from God and who can speak to what Christianity is.** Modern readers, seekers after a new code and story, have reversed the imagery and turned the text into one about gender roles.[54]

One other text casts Mary Magdalene as the "apostle of the apostles." It is from the church father Hippolytus, who lived around AD 170–236. He says that Mary is the "apostle of the apostles," yet the version of his work that includes this phrase does not even appear until the tenth century. Even in this version, the word "apostle" is not used in the same sense as that which refers to the original twelve apostles. Hippolytus was writing about the women (plural) who were witnesses at the tomb. All of them, not just Mary, were apostles (plural) to the apostles. Hippolytus was not using "apostles" in the technical sense of church office. Rather, he used the everyday meaning of the word as someone who is commissioned with a message, speaking on behalf of another. These women were apostles sent by Jesus to deliver a message to the apostles—mainly that He had risen from the dead. In that sense, Hippolytus says they were apostles to the apostles, not in the sense of church office. For *The Da Vinci Code* to argue such a view from this late text certainly lacks credibility, directly conflicting with the authors of the New Testament.

THE FACTS

> *Consequently, you are no longer foreigners and aliens, but fellow citizens with God's people and members of God's household, built on the foundation of the apostles and prophets, with Christ Jesus himself as the chief cornerstone.* EPHESIANS 2:19–20

So what *does* the Bible say about the role of Mary Magdalene? Many throughout history have claimed Mary was a prostitute or even married to Jesus, as earlier discussed. However, the first time we read about Mary Magdalene in the Bible is in Luke 8:1–3. We read:

> Now it came to pass, afterward, that He went through every city and village, preaching and bringing the glad tidings of the kingdom of God. And the twelve were with Him, and certain women who had been healed of evil spirits and infirmities—Mary called Magdalene, out of whom had come seven demons, and Joanna the wife of Chuza, Herod's steward, and Susanna, and many others who provided for Him from their substance. (NKJV)

A clear reading of the text offers nothing that could be taken as evidence that Mary was a prostitute. How did this idea come about? Professor Ben Witherington explains:

> It is important to stress where she first appears in the Gospels, because by the Middle Ages there had long been a confusion about who she was. The anonymous sinner woman mentioned in Luke 7, who anointed Jesus' feet in the house of Simon the Pharisee, was assumed to be Miriam of Magdala [Mary Magdalene]. This is a serious mistake, and it really only became possible to make this mistake once manuscripts of the New Testament began to appear with separations of words, sentences, paragraphs, and then chapters and verses. That process first happened in the early Middle Ages.[55]

In this instance, *The Da Vinci Code*'s account is accurate. A close reading of the gospels shows no mention of Mary Magdalene as a prostitute. The first mention of Mary as a prostitute originates from a sermon delivered by Pope Gregory the Great in AD 591.

The next scriptural reference to Mary Magdalene describes her as one who is watching Jesus at the cross along with several other people (MATTHEW 27:55–56; MARK 15:40; JOHN 19:25). After Christ's death, Mary is also among those who witnessed the burial of Jesus (MATTHEW 27:61; MARK 15:40). Then, on the first Easter morning, Mary and some other women walked to Christ's grave, becoming the first witnesses to the resurrection (MATTHEW 28:1; MARK 16:1; JOHN 20:11–18).

In John 20:11–18 Jesus and Mary Magdalene were alone together after His resurrection. She clings to Jesus because of her astonishment at seeing Him, but Jesus tells her to let go. No sexual intimacy is implied in the account. The story concludes with her leaving the scene in great joy and excitement at Jesus' being alive.

The New Testament tells us nothing more of Mary Magdalene's life. Though it is clear from these references that she was a devoted follower of Jesus, we can state with certainty that Mary Magdalene's relationship with Jesus was nothing beyond that of a disciple following her Master.

In speaking about Mary Magdalene's role in the early church, discuss with others:

✓ What do you think of the way *The Da Vinci Code* discusses Mary Magdalene?

✓ How much do you think is true about the way *The Da Vinci Code* portrays Mary Magdalene?

✓ What have you read from the New Testament about Mary Magdalene?

✓ Do you know the true story of Mary? Would you be willing to talk about it (or read about it) together?

FACT #10

Jesus Always Claimed to Be God

"At this gathering [the Council of Nicaea]," Teabing said, "many aspects of Christianity were debated and voted upon . . . [including] the divinity of Jesus."

[Sophie] "I don't follow. His divinity?"

*"My dear," Teabing declared, "until that moment in history, Jesus was viewed by His followers as a mortal prophet . . . a great and powerful man, but a man nonetheless. **A mortal.**"*

"Not the Son of God?"

*"Right," Teabing said. "Jesus' establishment as 'the Son of God' was officially **proposed and voted on** by the Council of Nicaea."*

"Hold on. You're saying Jesus' divinity was the result of a vote?"

*"A **relatively close vote** at that," Teabing added.* (DVC, 233)

Is it true that the divinity of Jesus was decided at the Council of Nicaea? Was there really a close vote? If not, what happened at this Council?

In discussing the above dialogue attacking the divine nature of Jesus, it is helpful to note what actually happened. The Council of Nicaea took place as a gathering of approximately 318 early church leaders in AD 325. Eusebius, a participant at this gathering, wrote back the following review to his local church:

We believe in One God, the Father Almighty, the Maker of all things visible and invisible. And in One Lord Jesus Christ, the Word of God, God from God, Light from Light, Life from Life, Son Only-begotten, first-born of every creature, before all the ages, begotten from the Father, by Whom also all things were made.... That this we have ever thought from our heart and soul, from the time we recollect ourselves, and now think and say in truth, before God Almighty and our Lord Jesus Christ do we witness, being able by proofs to show and to convince you, that, **even in times past, such has been our belief and preaching.**

Eusebius' conclusion was that the Council merely affirmed what the church had always believed and taught about Jesus' divinity. The Council didn't invent His divinity. Instead, the life and message of Jesus inspired the Nicene Creed.

THE FICTION

*"The early Church needed to convince the world that the **mortal prophet** Jesus was a divine being. Therefore, any gospels that described earthly aspects of Jesus' life had to be omitted from the Bible."* (DVC, 244)

As we have seen, the Council of Nicaea gathered to settle a dispute regarding the relationship of Jesus to God the Father. Arius, a church leader in Alexandria, argued that Jesus was a created being of a different substance than the Father. Arius actively promoted his views, delivering letters to several churches. Constantine called the Council of Nicaea so bishops could settle the controversy and build unity throughout the empire.

Athanasius set forth the historic view that Jesus was of the same divine substance as the Father and therefore fully divine. All but two of over three hundred bishops sided with Athanasius, because they had long already held this view. The claim that Jesus was not recognized as God until the fourth century is historically baseless. The vast majority of historians recognize that Jesus' divinity was taught by Jesus and His apostles from the late AD 20s to AD 75.

THE FACTS

> *By Him all things were created, both in the heavens and on earth, visible and invisible, whether thrones or dominions or rulers or authorities—**all things have been created through Him and for Him.*** (COLOSSIANS 1:16, NASB)

In addition to the New Testament's clear teaching that Christ was both human and divine, the writings of the early church fathers help prove that the early church fully believed that Jesus Christ was God long before the Council of Nicaea:[58]

Ignatius (50–115): In *To the Ephesians* and other letters, we find references such as the following: "Jesus Christ our God"; "who is God and man"; "received knowledge of God, that is, Jesus Christ"; "for our God, Jesus the Christ"; "for God was manifest as man"; "Christ, who was from eternity with the Father"; "from God, from Jesus Christ"; "from Jesus Christ, our God"; "Our God, Jesus Christ"; "suffer me to follow the example of the passion of my God"; "Jesus Christ the God"; and "Our God Jesus Christ."

Polycarp (69–155): Spoke of "Our Lord and God Jesus Christ."

Justin Martyr (100–165): "[Jesus] who . . . being the first-begotten Word of God, is even God." In his *Dialogue with Trypho,* he stated that "God was born from a virgin" and that Jesus was "worthy of worship" and of being "called Lord and God."

Tatian (?–170): "We do not act as fools, O Greeks, nor utter idle tales when we announce that God was born in the form of man."

Irenaeus (130–202): Jesus was "perfect God and perfect man . . . not a mere man . . . but was very God . . . He is in Himself in His own right . . . God, and Lord, and King Eternal."

Tertullian (160–220): "Christ is also God [because] that which has come forth from God is at once God and the Son of God, and the two are one . . . in His birth, God and man united."

Caius (180–217): "Who is ignorant of the books of Irenaeus and Melito, and the rest, which declare Christ to be God and man? All the psalms, too, and hymns of brethren, which have been written from the beginning by the faithful, celebrate Christ the Word of God, ascribing divinity to Him. . . . [This] doctrine of the Church, then, has been proclaimed so many years ago."

Gregory Thaumaturgus (210–260): "All [the persons] are one nature, one essence, one will, and are called the Holy Trinity; and these also are names subsistent, one nature in three persons, and one genus [kind]."

Novatian (200–258): "He was also God according to the Scriptures. . . . Scripture has as much described Jesus Christ to be man, as moreover it has also described Christ the Lord to be God."

Athanasius (293–373): "[Jesus] always was and is God and Son. . . . He who is eternally God . . . also became man for our sake."

From the New Testament apostles through the time of the Council of Nicaea, virtually all Christians held to the view that Jesus was both human and divine. *The Da Vinci Code*'s argument that Christ's divinity was invented in the fourth century is thought by most historians as bizarre and wrong.

In speaking with others about the divinity and humanity of Christ, ask:

✓ If you were asked to choose whether Jesus was Lord, legend, liar, or lunatic, which would you choose? Why? What do you personally think of Jesus?

✓ How much of what *The Da Vinci Code* says about Jesus is true?

✓ What have you read about Jesus from the Bible yourself? Would you be willing to read some of the gospels together? Could we talk more about my relationship to Jesus?

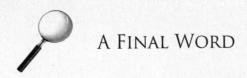

A FINAL WORD

In Lee Strobel's discussion guide *Exploring The Da Vinci Code*, he shares the following actual airplane conversation that took place between two individuals:

> **Passenger 1:** You're a Christian too? So am I.
> That's great.
> **Passenger 2:** Yeah, that's great. (pause)
>
> **Passenger 1:** I just read *The Da Vinci Code*.
> Have you read it?
> **Passenger 2:** Sure did.
>
> **Passenger 1:** What percentage do you think is true?
> **Passenger 2:** Oh, about 80 percent.[57]

Dan Brown may have created an absorbing novel that keeps you turning the pages. The movie may be exciting and well acted. But: *The Da Vinci Code*, more than anything, is an attack on historic Christianity. To fictionalize, trivialize, and invent is one thing. But to claim *The Da Vinci Code* as historical truth—to attack the person and work of Jesus Christ—is a challenge we cannot let go unchecked.

Why is it hard to remain neutral about Jesus? Why cannot people simply "leave Jesus alone"? It is hard to remain neutral about who this Jesus is because in the text of the Bible He claims to be God. He's not a little God, He's not semi-God and He's not even a representative of God; He is God. Jesus Christ is not a character with whom we can play fast and loose. Even a casual reader of the Bible comes to a juncture where he or she has to decide. If Jesus is who He said He is, did what He said He did, and was verified by hundreds or even thousands of eyewitnesses, a person has to decide. If you decide to disagree, ignore, or dismiss it out of hand, then you will stand now—and for eternity—based on your decision. This is why we believe each person has to come to terms with who this Jesus is.

We believe that Christ is the Son of God, born to die that man might live. We believe that only in His finished work can anyone find forgiveness and a relationship with Him. We believe that Jesus loves us and was willing to come to die in our place so we could live forever with Him. And it is His love that compels us to share His life, death, burial, and resurrection.

While Dan Brown may have tried to dismantle biblical Christianity, Jesus came to rescue us from do-it-yourself, man-made religion. While many authors have and will try to destroy the work of Christ, it is He who came to deal with sin and invite all people into relationship with Him.

As you discuss *The Da Vinci Code*, whether on an airplane, at the office, school, the gym, the boardroom, or local coffee shop, remember Paul's instruction to speak the truth in love (EPHESIANS 4:15). Do not fear speaking out about what you believe. And as you speak, speak of Jesus. Point to Him. We believe there is intrinsic power in the story of Jesus and His love. We do not have to know all answers to *The Da Vinci Code* or any other attack on Jesus Christ. We know Jesus. We believe He wants us to speak of Him so others may hear. Yet He also values our love for every person we encounter, whether they wholeheartedly agree with our values, mock our beliefs . . . or simply want to ask questions.

Ultimately, Jesus surrendered His rights for a cross of wood in order to show the power of His great love for all humanity. As you live out your faith, show grace, act in love, and speak with wisdom concerning the things God says are true. We pray God greatly uses you to help shape hearts and minds for Christ. May God bless you in your efforts to share the words of life!

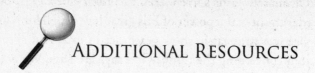

Additional Resources

Several additional books exist that respond to the controversies within *The Da Vinci Code* novel and film. We've included a complete list of books written from a Christian orientation to assist in your learning. However, please note we do not necessarily endorse the authors or views mentioned. These are simply listed for your research on this significant cultural and spiritual issue.

Abanes, Richard. *The Truth Behind The Da Vinci Code: A Challenging Response to the Bestselling Novel.* Eugene, OR: Harvest House Publishers, 2004.

Boa, Kenneth, and John Alan. *The Gospel According to The Da Vinci Code: The Truth Behind the Writings of Dan Brown.* Nashville, TN: Broadman & Holman, 2006.

Bock, Darrell L. *Breaking The Da Vinci Code: Answers to the Questions Everyone's Asking.* Nashville: Thomas Nelson, 2004.

Clark, Stephen. *The Da Vinci Code on Trial.* UK: Evangelical Press, 2006.

Ehrman, Bart D. *Truth and Fiction in The Da Vinci Code: A Historian Reveals What We Really Know about Jesus, Mary Magdalene and Constantine.* Oxford: Oxford University Press, 2004.

Flory, Susy, Gini Monroe, and W. Ward Gasque, *Fear Not Da Vinci: Using the Best-Selling Novel to Share Your Faith.* Chattanooga, TN: AMG Publishers, 2006.

Garlow, James L., and Peter Jones. *Cracking Da Vinci's Code: You've Read the Fiction, Now Read the Facts.* Colorado Springs: Victor/Cook Communications, 2004.

Garlow, James L., and Peter Jones. *Cracking Da Vinci's Code: Abridged Edition.* Colorado Springs, CO: Victor/Cook Communications, 2005.

Gilvin, Brandon. *Solving the Da Vinci Code Mystery*. Atlanta: Chalice Press, 2004.

Green, Michael. *The Books the Church Suppressed: Fiction and Truth in The Da Vinci Code*. Grand Rapids: Kregel, 2006.

Hanegraaff, Hank, and Paul L. Maier. *The Da Vinci Code: Fact or Fiction*.

Jones, Greg. *Beyond Da Vinci*. New York: Church Publishing Inc., 2004.

Kellmeyer, Steve. *Fact and Fiction in The Da Vinci Code*. Peoria, IL: Bridegroom Press, 2004.

Lutzer, Erwin W. *The Da Vinci Deception*. Wheaton, IL: Tyndale, 2004.

McDowell, Josh. *The Da Vinci Code: A Quest for Answers*. Holiday, FL: Green Key Books, 2006.

Newman, Sharan. *The Real History Behind The Da Vinci Code*. New York: Penguin Putnam Inc., 2005.

Olson, Carl E. and Sandra Miesel. *The Da Vinci Hoax: Exposing the Errors in The DaVinci Code*. Ft. Collins, CO: Ignatius Press, 2004.

Palmer, Adam, and Jeff Dunn. *Cracking Da Vinci's Code: Student Edition*. Colorado Springs: Cook Communications, 2006.

Strobel, Lee and Gary Pool. *Discussing The Da Vinci Code—DVD Curriculum*. Grand Rapids: Zondervan, 2006.

Strobel, Lee and Gary Pool. *Exploring The Da Vinci Code*. Grand Rapids: Zondervan, 2006.

Welborn, Amy. *De-coding Da Vinci: The Facts behind the Fiction of The Da Vinci Code*, Hunington, IN: Our Sunday Visitor, Inc., 2004.

Witherington III, Ben. *The Gospel Code: Novel Claims about Jesus, Mary Magdalene and Da Vinci*. Downers Grove: InterVarsity Press, 2004.

_____. PowerPoint *Answers to The Da Vinci Code*. Torrance, CA: Rose Publishing, 2006.

www.johnankerberg.org
www.christianitytoday.com
www.sermoncentral.com
www.outreach.com
www.leaderu.com/focus/davincicode.html
www.bible.org
www.moody.edu

ABOUT THE AUTHORS

Dr. Michael Easley (*BSEd, Stephen F. Austin University; ThM, DMin, Dallas Theological Seminary*) is president of Moody Bible Institute and the radio voice for the internationally syndicated *Proclaim!* broadcast. A veteran pastor with over twenty years in local church leadership experience, he is author of *Interludes* and serves as a frequent speaker for Family Life's marriage conferences. Michael is a graduate of Dallas Theological Seminary and lives in the Chicago area with his wife, Cindy, and their four children.

Dr. John Ankerberg (*BA, University of Illinois; MA, MDiv, Trinity Evangelical Divinity School; DMin, Luther Rice Seminary*) serves as host of the award-winning, nationally televised apologetic program *The John Ankerberg Show* and is president of The Ankerberg Theological Research Institute (www.johnankerberg.org). An internationally known speaker and radio personality, John has authored over seventy books, including the best-selling *Fast Facts On* series.

Dillon Burroughs is a freelance writer and editor. A graduate of Dallas Theological Seminary, he lives in the Indianapolis, Indiana, area with his wife, Deborah, and children.

ENDNOTES

THE FACTS BEHIND THE FICTION

1. Transcript from *The John Ankerberg Show, Answering the Questions Raised by The Da Vinci Code*, 2005.
2. Erwin Lutzer, *The Da Vinci Deception* (Wheaton, IL: Tyndale, 2004), xxv.
3. Dan Brown, interview by Matt Lauer, *The Today Show*, NBC, 9 June 2003.
4. David Klinghoffer, "Books, Arts and Manners," *National Review* (8 December 2003).

FACT #1: THE BIBLE IS COMPLETE AND ACCURATE

5. George Barna, *The Bible*, The Barna Group, www.barna.org/FlexPage.aspx?Page=Topic&TopicID=7.
6. A good way to think of a fragment is like a torn piece of parchment with writing that is still legible. We have literally thousands of fragments that confirm the Bible's reliability.
7. The Nag Hammadi includes twelve documents that are named after the location where they were discovered in Upper Egypt, Hamra Doum. These texts are Coptic, an ancient Egyptian language.
8. Gnosticism is a derived from a Greek word for knowledge, *Gnosis*. Historically, Gnostic writings and Gnostic teachings were considered heretical. In the last century, interest and scholarship in these so-called Gnostic texts have created a wide spectrum of ideas. At the foundation, Gnostic proponents exaggerate a "secret knowledge," dualism (matter is evil), and the need for enlightenment. The seductive nature of something "secretive" heightens interest in these Gnostic documents.
9. See Norman Geisler, www.johnankerberg.org/Articles/_PDFArchives/theological–dictionary/TD3W0402.pdf.
10. Frederick Kenyon, *The Bible and Archaeology* (New York, 1940), 288–289.
11. Norman Geisler and William Nix, *A General Introduction to the Bible* (Chicago: Moody, 1978), 134.
12. For other passages which either declare or assume the Bible as God's Word, see Deuteronomy 6:6–9, 17–18; Joshua 1:8–9; 8:32–35; 2 Samuel 22:31; Psalms 1:2; 12:6; 19:7–11; 93:5; 119:9, 11, 18, 89–93, 130; Proverbs 30:5–6;

Matthew 5:17–19; 22:29; Mark 13:31; Luke 16:17; John 2:22; 5:24; 10:35; Acts 17:11; Romans 10:17; Colossians 3:16; 1 Thessalonians 2:13; 2 Timothy 2:15; 3:15–17; 1 Peter 1:23–25; 2 Peter 3:15–16; Revelation 1:2; 22:18.

13. Charles C. Ryrie, *A Survey of Bible Doctrine* (Chicago: Moody, 1972), 38.
14. Complete citation of the church fathers in this section can be obtained at www.ankerberg.com/Articles/historical–Jesus/DaVinci/HJ–davinci–crash–davinci–code.htm
15. Kurt Aland, *The Problem of the New Testament Canon* (London: Mowbray, 1962), 18.
16. The following section is adapted from Dr. Ron Rhodes, "Crash Goes The Da Vinci Code," http://www.ankerberg.com/Articles/historical–Jesus/DaVinci/HJ–davinci–crash–davinci–code.htm.
17. Norman Geisler, "The Canonicity of the Bible," http://www.ankerberg.com/Articles/historical–Jesus/DaVinci/HJ–davinci–the–canonicity–of–the–Bible.htm.
18. Norman Geisler, editor, *Baker Encyclopedia of Christian Apologetics* (Grand Rapids: Baker 1999), 80–81. See also Norman Geisler, www.johnankerberg.org/Articles/_PDFArchives/theological–dictionary/TD1W0402.pdf.

FACT #2: JESUS NEVER MARRIED

19. Transcript from *The John Ankerberg Show*, "Answering the Questions Raised by *The Da Vinci Code*", 2005.
20. Hank Hanegraaff and Paul Maier, *The Da Vinci Code: Fact or Fiction* (Wheaton: Tyndale, 2004), 18.
21. Coptic refers to an ancient Egyptian language used in liturgical settings.
22. Ben Witherington, *The Gospel Code: Novel Claims about Jesus, Mary Magdalene and Da Vinci* (Downers Grove, IL: InterVarsity Press, 2004), 36.
23. Ibid., 24.
24. Darrell Bock, *Breaking The Da Vinci Code* (Nashville: Thomas Nelson, 2004), 23.
25. Erwin Lutzer, *The Da Vinci Deception* (Wheaton, IL: Tyndale, 2004), 55.
26. Matthew 4:1–11; Mark 1:12–13; Luke 4:1–13.

FACT #3: CHRISTIANITY DID NOT EMERGE FROM MYSTERY RELIGIONS

27. Erwin Lutzer, *The Da Vinci Deception* (Wheaton, IL: Tyndale, 2004), 128.
28. Ron Nash, "Was the New Testament Influenced by Pagan Religions?" *Christian Research Journal*, August 1994.
29. John Ankerberg, "What People Want to Know Most About *The Da Vinci Code*," *Ankerberg Theological Research Journal*: Special Edition, 2005, pg. 44.
For a full discussion of this see, John Ankerburg and Weldon, *The Passion of the Empty Tomb*, Appendix C, "The Ressurection of the Christ and the Mystery Religions", Eugene, OR: Harvest House Publishers, 2005.

30. Ibid.
31. The following section is adapted from J. Hampton Keathley III, *The Uniqueness of Jesus Christ*, www.bible.org/page.asp?page_id=538.
32. From the Biblical Studies Foundation, http://www.bible.org/category.asp?CategoryI D=90&ParentID=0&scid=1.
33. C.S. Lewis, *Miracles: A Preliminary Study* (London: Collins/Fontana, 1970), 119.

FACT #4: THE HIDDEN GOSPELS ARE NOT REALLY GOSPELS

34. Norman L. Geisler, *Baker Encyclopedia of Christian Apologetics* (Grand Rapids: Baker, 1999), 187.
35. "Discerning Fact from Fiction in *The Da Vinci Code*," http://www.evidenceandan-swers.com.
36. Ibid.
37. Craig L. Blomberg, Ph.D., Review of *The Da Vinci Code* in *Denver Journal, An Online Review of Current Biblical and Theological Studies*, http://www.denversemi-nary.edu/dj/articles2004/0200/0202.php.
38. Gleason Archer, *A Survey of Old Testament Introduction* (Chicago: Moody, 1964), 19.

FACT #5: CONSTANTINE DIDN'T INVENT THE NEW TESTAMENT

39. An "apology" in this sense means a formal defense of something.
40. Harold O.J. Brown, *Heresies* (Grand Rapids: Baker, 1984), 117.
41. Steve Brandt, *Council of Nicaea*, http://www.columbia.edu/cu/augustine/arch/sbrandt/Nicaea.htm
42. Bart Ehrman, *Truth and Fiction in The Da Vinci Code* (London: Oxford Univ. Press, 2004), 26.
43. F.F. Bruce, *The New Testament Documents: Are They Reliable?* (5th ed. Leicester: InterVarsity Press, 1959). Online version accessed at www.bible-researcher.com/bruce1.html.
44. Erwin Lutzer, *The Da Vinci Deception* (Wheaton, IL: Tyndale 2004), 93.
45. F.F. Bruce, *The Canon of Scripture* (Downers Grove, IL: InterVarsity, 1988), 160.

FACT #6: FAITH IS NOT BUILT ON FABRICATION

46. J. Richard Pearcey, *Boundless Webzine*, 2004, http://www.boundless.org/departments/pages/a0000882.html.

FACT #7: CHRISTIANITY EMBRACES THE RIGHTS OF WOMEN

47. Erwin Lutzer, *The Da Vinci Deception* (Wheaton, IL: Tyndale 2004), 102.
48. *The Nag Hammadi Library*, ed. James M. Robinson (San Francisco: Harper & Row, 1978), 130.
49. Ron Rhodes, "Crash Goes the *Da Vinci Code*," www.ronrhodes.org/DaVinci.html

FACT #8: SEX WAS NOT A METHOD TO COMMUNICATE WITH GOD

50. *Britannica Concise Encyclopedia* from Encyclopedia Britannica Premium Service, www.britannica.com/ebc/article?tocId=9367077, s.v. "hieras gamos"

FACT #9: MARY MAGDALENE WAS NOT INTENDED TO REPLACE PETER

51. See word study of the Greek, Hebrew, and Aramaic translations in C. Gordon Olson's Paper entitled "Gospel Proclamation on God's Terms" presented to the Evangelical Theological Society, 1997.
52. Ron Rhodes, "Crash Goes *The Da Vinci Code*," http://www.ankerberg.com/Articles/historical-Jesus/DaVinci/HJ-davinci-crash-davinci-code.htm.
53. Erwin Lutzer, *The Da Vinci Deception* (Wheaton, IL: Tyndale , 2004), 110.
54. Darrell L. Bock, *Breaking The Da Vinci Code* (Nashville: Thomas Nelson, 2004), 147.
55. Ben Witherington III, "Mary, Mary, Extraordinary," www.leaderu.com/theology/maryandjesus.html.

FACT #10: JESUS ALWAYS CLAIMED TO BE GOD

56. From www.ccel.org/fathers/NPNF2-04/v2/A3.HTM. All of these quotes are fully cited at: www.ankerberg.com/Articles/historical-Jesus/DaVinci/HJ-davinci-5-questions.htm

A FINAL WORD

57. Lee Strobel and Gary Poole, *Exploring The Da Vinci Code* (Grand Rapids: Zondervan, 2006), 7.